100 List Building

Methods

Terms and Conditions
LEGAL NOTICE

Introduction

This ebook will give you 100 list building methods. It contains ideas for freebies and copywriting strategies that will persuade people to subscribe to your opt-list or e-mail newsletter. Building a huge opt-in list can give you income anytime you want by just pushing the send button.

1. One can conclude you can endorse a free sample. This will add additional list customers. You could persuade prospects to opt-in after showing off your freebie product cover/graphic.

2. It is my belief, you should release free brandable rights. This will create extra opt-in fans. You may influence prospects to join by bringing up the professional writer you hired to create the product.

3. I happen to believe you could publicize a free membership. It might construct you some new subscriber traffic. You could bribe visitors to reserve their spot by broadcasting you are offering an affiliate contest.

4. The best I can tell you is you might offer a free customer forum. This should grow your list. You might bring leads to get your freebie after cataloging that you have excellent affiliate tools.

5. In broad terms, you can give away a free ecourse. It could dig up additional email customers. You should bring people around to accept your deal, by certifying you have subscriber testimonials.

6. A case can be made that you may present a free video. This may drive more list clients to you. You can budge prospects to approve your offer via chiming in, that you have a secure opt-in system

7. Some have claimed you should market a free audio. It would increase your subscriber referrals. You may conjure visitors to enroll by claiming it takes seconds/minutes to get it.

8. It is quite clear you could advertise a free excerpt. This should enrich your email income. You could captivate leads to register by commenting you have unsolicited testimonial.

9. It is no coincidence that you might promote a free trial. It can ensure new list buyers. You might cause people to subscribe by communicating proof it works with your test results.

10. As a general rule you should advertise a free day trial pass. This should flood your opt-in network. You may persuade leads to click enter by repeating they get it for nada/zip/zilch/diddly-squat.

11. You could plug a free newsletter. It might extend your opt-in shoppers. You can charm visitors to click submit by confirming the list of benefits.

12. You could give away a free quick start guide. It can accelerate your subscribers. You could persuade people to subscribe by posting the original price it sold for.

13. Consider launching free software. This should fortify more email endorsers. You may coach leads to click enter by conveying you have audio/video testimonials.

14. I would contend that you could pitch free articles. It could fill up a lot of subscriptions. You could coax people to sign up by telling them the words your freebie won.

15. It is my contention you might release a free booklet. This may gain extra list advertisers. You might command prospects to fill in their info with defining your business is polite and professional.

16. There is no doubt, you can publicize a free classified ad. It would generate new subscriber clicks. You should condition visitors to apply to your list from demonstrating the freebie was beta tested.

17. It is important to emphasize you may offer a free consulting. This shall grab additional email spenders. You can contribute to leads to enlist after describing the freebie is ending soon.

18. It is encouraging to note you should give away free distribution rights. It can develop your ezine admirers. You may convert people to type their info by detailing your professional credentials.

19. The evidence shows you could present free email consolidation. This will give you more subscriber resellers. You could convince prospects to join by disclosing the freebie's case studies.

20. You might want to market free email support. It might increase your email supporters. You might direct visitors to reserve their spot through discussing it beats competitors paid product.

21. Examining the issue you can advertise a free ezine. This should heighten your list of advocates. You should draw leads to get your freebie by providing screen shots that the freebie works.

22. As one might expect, you may promote a free ezine submission. It could help get new email viewers. You can drive people to accept your deal from saying they are making the right choice.

23. It is apparent that you might present a free report. This will acquire you more readers. You might allure prospects to opt-in by adding they will get 50% commission.

24. In my experience, you should endorse a free gift. This may implement additional subscriber hits. You may affect prospects to approve your offer after divulging how much money it took to create it.

25. To a certain extent, you could plug a free gift subscription. It would increase your readership. You could enchant visitors to enroll by documenting frequently asked questions.

26. By examining further you might launch a free web cam access. This should improve your click-through list. You might encourage leads to register by announcing that only so many freebies are left.

27. The simple fact is you can pitch a free lesson. It can influence opt-in partners. You could subscribe through establishing that it's never been released before.

28. It is appropriate to mention you may release free personal help. This will inspire extra co-ops to subscribe. You can enlist prospects to opt-in while exhibiting they will have immediate/instant access to it.

29. A fair assumption is you should publicize free publicity. It might intensify your email viewers. You may entice visitors to click submit by explaining they should view your countdown counter.

30. You could offer free reprint rights. This should add additional subscriber conversions. You could entrap leads to click enter after specifying you only offer it once a season/year.

31. You could give away free tools. It could lengthen your open rates. You might sign people up by expressing their subscription info will remain confidential.

32. You can offer free shipping. This may maintain you more list contacts. You should encourage prospects to fill in their information.

33. You may want to market a free subscription. It would make you tons of opt-in colleagues. You can influence visitors to apply through highlighting all the myths and misconceptions.

34. Don't dismiss marketing a free checklist. It might add you numerous email friends. You can alter visitors to click submit by saying you have 24/customer/tech service.

35. You could also advertise free support. This shall manage to get you extra list admirers. You may fascinate leads to enlist by telling your subscriber's success stories.

36. It is generally presumed you could promote free telephone consulting. It can maximize new opt-in browsers. You could drive people to type their info from demonstrating it's fully guaranteed to work.

37. As a general rule, you might endorse free advertising. This will modify additional subscriber supporters. You might get prospects to join after suggesting they can unsubscribe any time.

38. You could plug a free contest entry. It might motivate email students to sign up. It should give way to visitors to reserve their spot by indexing they have to sign a non-disclosure agreement to get it.

39. You could launch a free sweepstakes entry. This should multiply your opt-in viewers. You can administer leads to get your freebie by supplying your personal/non-business credentials.

40. You should pitch free lifetime updates. It could obtain numerous list linkers. You may guide people to accept your deal through insisting it's easy to use.

41. You could release a free extended warranty. This may increase your subscriber acquaintances. You could encourage prospects to approve your offer by revealing it is full of examples.

42. You might publicize a free contact list. It would persuade new email connections. You might hook visitors to enroll by listing it has, many helpful links.

43. You can offer a free service. This shall preserve additional readership revenue. You should pursue leads to register after stating its 100% original information.

44. You could give away free graphics. It can prolong your list royalties. You can convince people to subscribe by making public it's in 3d/high definition.

45. You could advertise a free ebook. This should assemble extra opt-in followers. You can appeal leads to click enter by advertising your educational background

46. My inclination is you should present a free gift certificate. This will protect your subscriber income. You may incite prospects to opt-in by saying a child could use/do it.

47. You could market a free coupon. It might raise your email sales. You could incline visitors to click submit through mentioning its custom designed/customizable.

48. For all intent and purposes, you might advertise a free webinar. This should increase your subscriber orders. You might persuade leads to click enter by mentioning It's very detailed.

49. You can promote a free teleseminars. It could create new opt-in payments for you. You should impose people to sign up from narrating it's a huge collection/or collectable.

50. You could endorse a free backlinks. This may regulate additional list wealth. You can influence prospects to fill in their info after noting it's a closely guarded secret weapon.

51. I suggest plugging free tech help. It would reinforce your email riches. You may inspire visitors to apply by inserting it's a valuable reference.

52. You could launch free content. This should make your opt-in profits better. You could lure leads to enlist by penciling in its very accurate.

53. You might want to pitch free add ons. It can seize you more list earnings. You might interest people to type their info through pointing out its adaptable/versatile

54. You could release free master rights. This will revise your money situation. You could give prospects a reason to join by presenting the add-ons they get with it.

55. You can publicize free private label rights. It might safeguard your subscription assets. You can launch visitors to reserve their spot by proclaiming it's patented/copyrighted/trademarked.

56. According to research, you should promote free consulting. It could attract a lot of new leads. You may rouse people to sign up by affirming your opt-in numbers and statistics.

57. In large part, you should offer a free e-class. This should secure you additional list cash flow. You may lead people to get your freebie after acknowledging it's been autographed.

58. You could give away a free workshop. It could load up your email bank account. You could lure people to accept your deal by promoting it's fully programmable.

59. You might offer a free instant commissions. This may strengthen more list investments. You might magnetize prospects to approve your offer by advertising its very compatible.

60. In the long run, you can market free surprise bonuses. It would stretch out your opt-in bank deposits. You can direct visitors to enroll through publishing it's crystal clear.

61. It has been said that you should advertise free mystery bonuses. This shall transform your email finances for the better. You can maneuver leads to register by telling them there's no wallet/credit card needed to get it.

62. You should promote free installation. It can upgrade your overall list funds. You may gesture people to subscribe by putting up it includes easy directions/instructions

63. A like-minded view is you could endorse a free JV program. This will win additional email income returns. You could motivate prospects to opt-in after relating it's up to date/constantly updating.

64. It makes sense that you might plug free 100% commissions. It might amplify your bottom line. You might move visitors to click submit by noting its newbie friendly

65. At any given time, you can launch a free fast start bonus. This should blow up your list income streams. You should negotiate leads to click enter by referencing its easy to install/set up.

66. You could pitch a free resource list bonus. It could boost your overall subscriber capital. You can persuade people to sign up through conveying it is easy to read.

67. You could endorse free training. This may rejuvenate your email prospects. You could assert prospects to fill in their opt-in info after disclosing it's a limited time offer.

68. In a manner of speaking, you should release free past experience stories. This may broaden your opt-in commissions. You may lead prospects to fill in their subscriber info by telling them it's proven and time tested.

69. You could publicize free transcripts. It would bulk up new email buyer transactions. You could pilot visitors to apply by announcing its uncut/uncensored.

70. You might want to offer a free teleseminar. This should widen your ezine circulation. You might propel leads to enlist after commenting it has expert contributors.

71. You can give away a free product critic. It could inflate your email wallet. You should prompt people to provide their info by reporting it has professionally designed graphics.

72. If I may mention, you may present a free photo gallery. This will swell your list pocket book. You can drive prospects to join revealing it downloads really fast/quick.

73. You should market a free sneak preview. It might widen your opt-in dollars. You may prompt visitors to reserve their spot by saying it's full of resources/links.

74. Let's keep in mind, you could advertise free interviews. This should spread out your email currency. You could pull leads to get your freebie by sharing it's fully searchable and easy to navigate.

75. You could promote a free future bonuses. It could escalate your financial numbers. You might motivate people to accept your deal from composing its glitch proof/error free.

76. You can endorse a free MLM program. This may skyrocket your list billfold. You should reassure prospects to accept your offer by speaking about its high quality.

77. You should plug free coaching. It would blossom your list sponsors. You can get visitors to enroll by specifying it's in details/specifics.

78. One can assume, you might promote a free seminar ticket. It would bolster your opt-ins. You might assure visitors to apply by announcing it took years/months to create.

79. Take note of the fact, you should launch a free audio version of your product. This should build up your email treasure. You may motivate leads to register via telling them it's mobile.

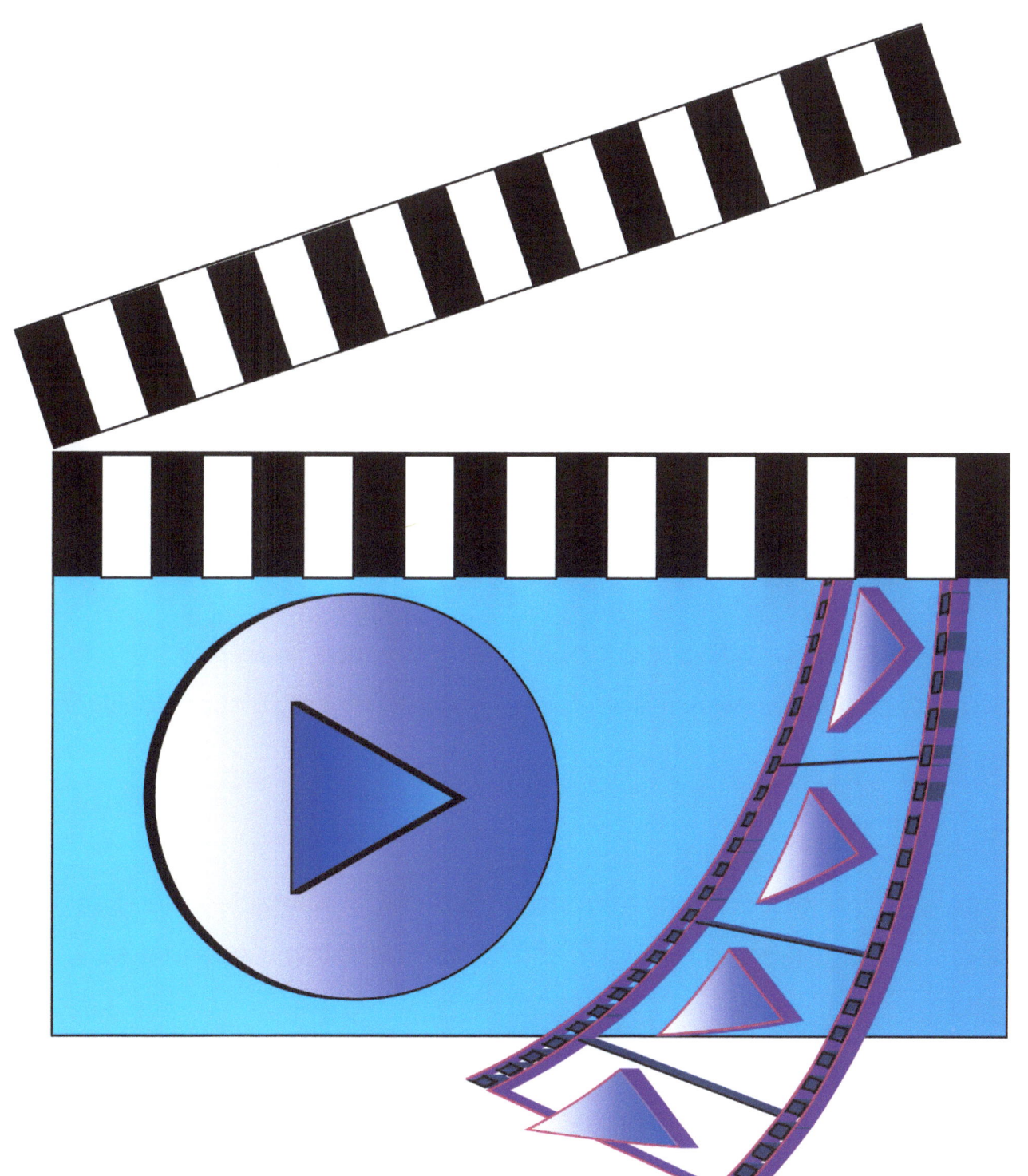

80. You could pitch a free video version. It can sprout your list's balance sheet. You could move people to subscribe through spilling it's highly organized.

81. You might release a free PDF version. This will erect you more subscriber payments. You might slide prospects to opt-in by stating there's no cost.

82. You can publicize free web site critiquing. It might accumulate your list pockets. You should encourage visitors to click submit from stipulating you'll foot the bill for it.

83. You can offer free two tier commissions. This should manufacture additional greenbacks. You can steer leads to click enter after submitting it's as free as air/dirt/birds.

84. You should give away a free affiliate forum. It could springboard new email affiliates. You may inspire people to sign up by suggesting there's no strings attached or obligations.

85. You could present a free physical backup copy. This may catapult your overall subscription purse. You could stir prospects to fill in their info by telling them that they don't need to spend any money.

86. You might market free templates. It would propel your checks from list clients. You might sway visitors to apply through telling them you removed the price tag/sticker.

87. You could advertise a free site replica. This shall advance you email bucks. You could swing leads to enlist with testifying they can skip the order button.

88. You could promote a free early bird bonuses. It can give you new opt-in spenders. You can tempt people to type their info from texting they can steal/swipe/rob them from you.

89. As you are aware you can launch free resell rights. This shall boost your list members. You might attract leads to enlist informing them of your list of famous subscribers.

90. You should endorse a free beta version. This will increase your subscriber patrons. You may trigger prospects to join after transmitting you will give so much money to charity for every opt-in.

91. You could plug a free demo. It might pull in extra opt-ins. You could entice visitors to reserve their spot by typing you removed/destroyed the order page.

92. You might launch a free certification test/license. This should surge your email participates. You might twist leads to get your freebie uncovering they have no risk.

93. You can pitch a free mastermind session. It could hike up your subscriber community. You can inspire people to accept your deal through unveiling it's a zero cost investment.

94. You could release a free brainstorm session. This may fill up your opt-in piggybank. You can urge prospects to accept your offer with uttering there are no up-sells/one-time-offers.

95. To make it simple you should publicize a free business tour. It would gather a lot of new list buying receipts. You may usher visitors to enroll from venting there's no hidden fees.

96. You could offer a free swipe file. This should maximize your email proceeds. You could warrant leads to register after voicing there's no forced continuity.

97. You should give away a free podcasts. It can deepen your list savings. You might move people to subscribe by vouching its 100% free and no charges.

98. You can present free toll free advice. This will add to your subscription fortune. You should win over prospects to opt-in by writing that you removed the order button.

99. You could market a free 3 day trial. It might shoot up your overall list circulation yield. You can wow visitors to click submit through replying it's not a trick or scam.

100. You could pitch a free content archive. It can build up your email visitors. You can influence people to type their opt-in info by giving a summary of everything included.

I hope these List Building Methods bring you great success! Watch for more of my eBooks on Internet marketing coming soon!

Best wishes,

Melanie Fell

www.ingramcontent.com/pod-product-compliance
Lightning Source LLC
Chambersburg PA
CBHW050818180526
45159CB00004B/1705